Overflowing
with
Gratitude

A 90-day journey to making Gratitude a lifestyle

Overflowing with Gratitude
Copyright © 2019 Gina Low

Gratitude, Self-Awareness, Self-Development, Personal Growth, Happiness

All rights reserved. No part of this book may be reproduced in any manner whatsoever, or stored in any information storage system, without the expressed written consent of the publisher or the author, except in the case of brief quotations with proper reference, embodied in critical articles and reviews.

Cover and interior design by Gina Low

All quotations remain the intellectual property of their respective originators. All use of quotations is done under the fair use copyright principal.

ISBN: 9781095824139

Printed in the United States of America

Disclaimer: This publication is sold with the understanding that the author is not engaged in rendering professional psychological services. If expert assistance or counseling is needed, the services of a competent professional should be sought.

We are what we repeatedly do.
Excellence, then, is not an act, but a
habit.

Aristotle

A word about habits
(and then a few more about Gratitude)

It is said that 21 days of consistent behavior will make or break a habit. Anybody that has struggled with addiction knows that the first 21 days is NEVER the end, and ALWAYS the hardest. It really is what you do every day after that creates a desired lifestyle. Scientific research now shows that an average of 60+ days of repetition is required for something to become habitual, and at least 90 days for auto-pilot to take over. Ninety days to create a lifestyle. Three months. One quarter of one year to create a drastically different lifestyle for yourself.

It's been just over three years since the idea of constant, and sometimes "fake it 'til I make it" gratitude has changed my life. It's not perfect; all my problems did not suddenly get washed away. What did change, however, was a drastic shift in my perception.

When your perception changes, your attitude changes.
When your attitude changes, your mindset changes.
When your mindset changes, the world around you changes, and you become an unstoppable force.

Maybe I am happier, more motivated, less negative, and thinking more clearly. Maybe the Universe has just aligned with the energy I now radiate, and continues to reflect it all back to me. Probably both. Either way, it's real, and I wish the same for you.

Your thoughts will determine the outcomes in your life. I invite you to embark on a 90-day adventure exploring your thoughts - begin to notice the little things that make you smile each day. Be thankful; be blessed.

Change your perception, change your attitude, change your mindset - Become Unstoppable.

Week 1

WEEK 1 _____ to _____

This week I am most excited about:
_____
_____
_____

"Today, I am grateful for…"

Monday
1. _____
2. _____
3. _____

Tuesday
#TalktomeTuesday – What's one kind or thoughtful thing someone did for you recently?
_____
_____

Wednesday
1. _____
2. _____
3. _____

Gratitude is Riches. Complaint is Poverty.

-Doris Day

Thursday

1. _____
2. _____
3. _____

Friday

1. _____
2. _____
3. _____

Saturday

1. _____
2. _____
3. _____

Sunday

1. _____
2. _____
3. _____

The BEST thing that happened in my life this week was:

_____
_____
_____

Confirm to the Universe that what you wish to manifest is *already yours.*

Energize the Law of Attraction by practicing **GRATITUDE NOW** *for things you wish to manifest in the future.*

Visualize and draw something you'll be grateful for when it arrives in the future.

Week 2

WEEK 2   _____ to _____

This week I am most excited about:

_____

_____

_____

"Today, I am grateful for…"

Monday
1. _____
2. _____
3. _____

Tuesday
#TalktomeTuesday – How have your spiritual beliefs or practices fulfilled you recently?

_____

_____

Wednesday
1. _____
2. _____
3. _____

This is a Wonderful Day. I've never seen this one before.

-Maya Angelou

Thursday

1. _____
2. _____
3. _____

Friday

1. _____
2. _____
3. _____

Saturday

1. _____
2. _____
3. _____

Sunday

1. _____
2. _____
3. _____

The BEST thing that happened in my life this week was:

_____
_____
_____

GRATITUDE in ACTION!

What are some ways you've been the lucky recipient of someone else's gratitude?

_____
_____
_____
_____
_____
_____
_____
_____

Ideas for blessing others with your own gratitude:

- Send a card or handwritten note.
- "Pay it forward" in line.
- Bring someone coffee.
- Look a stranger in the eyes and smile.
- Ask someone about the best part of their day.
- Mow the neighbor's lawn.
- Take someone's children to the park.
- Give someone an extra-long hug.
- Deliver flowers just to brighten someone's day.
- Offer to return someone's shopping cart.
- Compliment 5 random people.
- Have dinner delivered to someone who's been busy (everyone likes pizza!)
- Bring tea, cough drops, magazines, etc. to someone who's feeling under the weather.
- Find one thing you can do to lighten someone's load today.

Week 3

WEEK 3 _____ to _____

This week I am most excited about:
_____
_____
_____

"Today, I am grateful for…"

Monday
1. _____
2. _____
3. _____

Tuesday
#TalktomeTuesday – *What simple pleasure did you enjoy today?*
_____
_____

Wednesday
1. _____
2. _____
3. _____

Give Thanks for a Little, and you will find A Lot.

-Hansa Proverb

Thursday

1. _____
2. _____
3. _____

Friday

1. _____
2. _____
3. _____

Saturday

1. _____
2. _____
3. _____

Sunday

1. _____
2. _____
3. _____

The BEST thing that happened in my life this week was:

_____
_____
_____

Scientifically-proven benefits of being grateful:

- ✓ Gratitude improves physical health.
- ✓ Gratitude improves relationships.
- ✓ Grateful people sleep better.
- ✓ Gratitude improves self-esteem.
- ✓ Grateful people are more motivated.
- ✓ Grateful people have more willpower.
- ✓ Gratitude improves mental strength.
- ✓ Grateful people experience more empathy.
- ✓ Gratitude reduces aggression.
- ✓ Gratitude increases coping skills.
- ✓ Grateful people are more open-minded.
- ✓ Gratitude reduces heart stress.
- ✓ Grateful people build stronger connections.
- ✓ Grateful people are more effective leaders.
- ✓ Gratitude spreads high-vibrational energy.
- ✓ Grateful people are less offens-ive.
- ✓ Grateful people are less offend-ed.
- ✓ Gratitude increases the release of dopamine and serotonin (your body's natural anti-depressant).

Manufacture *Gratitude Triggers*

Sometimes you won't feel grateful. Sometimes you'll feel busy, and stressed, and overwhelmed. You can build a trigger(s) into your environment that will immediately return your soul to its circle of gratitude.

Choose an object that immediately brings you joy when you see it. It doesn't have to be fancy – it can be a rock painted with your favorite color, a family photo, or a keepsake from your last vacation. Place that object somewhere in your home and/or work environment. Seeing this object triggers your neurotransmitters and raises your vibrational energy to Grateful. An attitude of gratitude will wax and wane, but can always be recalled from your inner being.

The more we activate Gratitude, the more our neural pathways recognize what is going *right* instead of always seeing the problem as the big picture. Luckily, the neuroplasticity of our brains gives us the ability to form new neural responses and drop destructive reactionary processes no longer being used. Gratitude begets Gratitude.

Week 4

WEEK 4   _____ to _____

This week I am most excited about:
_____
_____
_____

"Today, I am grateful for…"

Monday
1. _____
2. _____
3. _____

Tuesday
#TalktomeTuesday – Have you had an opportunity to help someone recently, and how did it make you feel?
_____
_____

Wednesday
1. _____
2. _____
3. _____

The Struggle Ends when Gratitude Begins.

-Neale Donald Walsh

Thursday

1. _____
2. _____
3. _____

Friday

1. _____
2. _____
3. _____

Saturday

1. _____
2. _____
3. _____

Sunday

1. _____
2. _____
3. _____

The BEST thing that happened in my life this week was:

_____
_____
_____

Soil-Enriching
Soul-Enriching
nutrients:

Kindness	Awareness
Gratitude	Faith
Self-care	Education
Patience	Adventure
Empathy	Compassion
Forgiveness	Desire
Physical Activity	Creativity
Reading	Hope
Rest	Communication

If your programming is in the roots, and your desired qualities manifested in the leaves, what nutrients will you put in the soil to feed your tree of life?

Gratitude

Choose at least 5 more, and add your own words to feed you tree with soul-enriching nutrients

Week 5

WEEK 5　　　_____ to _____

This week I am most excited about:

_____

_____

_____

"Today, I am grateful for…"

Monday

1. _____

2. _____

3. _____

Tuesday

#TalktomeTuesday – What choice have you made in the last five years that you'd thank yourself for making?

_____

_____

Wednesday

1. _____

2. _____

3. _____

Appreciation in advance brings everything you want to you.

-Abraham Hicks

Thursday
1. _____
2. _____
3. _____

Friday
1. _____
2. _____
3. _____

Saturday
1. _____
2. _____
3. _____

Sunday
1. _____
2. _____
3. _____

The BEST thing that happened in my life this week was:
_____
_____
_____

ILLUSTRATE:

What would

Double the Happiness

look like to you?

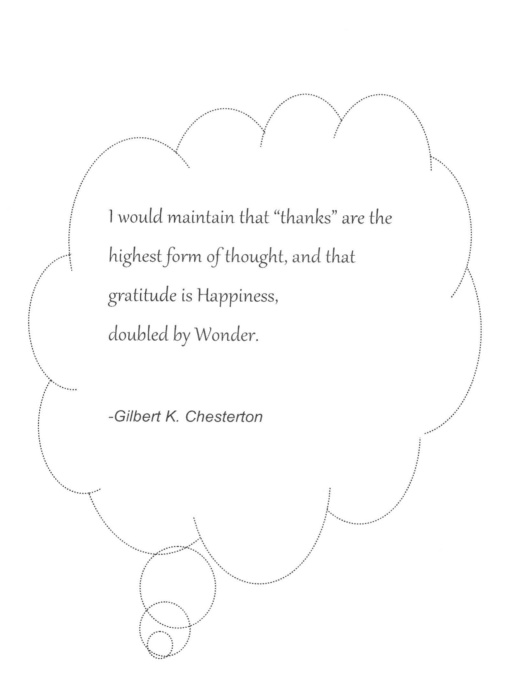

I would maintain that "thanks" are the highest form of thought, and that gratitude is Happiness, doubled by Wonder.

-Gilbert K. Chesterton

Week 6

WEEK 6 _____ to _____

This week I am most excited about:

_____
_____
_____

"Today, I am grateful for…"

Monday
1. _____
2. _____
3. _____

Tuesday
#TalktomeTuesday – What's the weather like today, and what's one good thing about that?
_____
_____

Wednesday
1. _____
2. _____
3. _____

If the only prayer you ever say in your entire life is "Thank You", it will be enough

--Meister Eckhart

Thursday
1._____
2._____
3._____

Friday
1._____
2._____
3._____

Saturday
1._____
2._____
3._____

Sunday
1._____
2._____
3._____

The BEST thing that happened in my life this week was:
_____
_____
_____

Rays of Joy

Mists of Hope

Fog of Peace

Showers of Blessings

Bolts of Energy

Winds of Change

What is the weather like right now?

_____
_____
_____

What about the weather do you enjoy?

_____
_____
_____

How does this weather make you feel?

_____
_____
_____

What does this weather make you want to do?

_____
_____
_____
_____
_____
_____

Week 7

WEEK 7 _____ to _____

This week I am most excited about:

_____

_____

_____

"Today, I am grateful for…"

Monday
1._____
2._____
3._____

Tuesday
#TalktomeTuesday – What activity, exercise or practice immediately improves your mood?

_____

_____

Wednesday
1._____
2._____
3._____

Thankfulness is the beginning of Gratitude. Gratitude is the completion of Thankfulness.

-Henri Frederic Amiel

Thursday
1._____
2._____
3._____

Friday
1._____
2._____
3._____

Saturday
1._____
2._____
3._____

Sunday
1._____
2._____
3._____

The BEST thing that happened in my life this week was:
_____
_____
_____

List 10 amenities that are readily available to you, but not so available to everyone else in the world.

1._____

2._____

3._____

4._____

5._____

6._____

7._____

8._____

9._____

10._____

Choose an item from your amenities list to visualize living WITHOUT.

Amenity_____

Would your life be more difficult or less difficult without this item? _____

How long do you think you would miss this item? _____

Look up a culture/demographic who lives without this item already. How do they "make do" without this amenity in their life?
_____

What do you think you will learn by living without this item?
_____

Week 8

WEEK 8 _____ to _____

This week I am most excited about:

_____
_____
_____

"Today, I am grateful for…"

Monday
1. _____
2. _____
3. _____

Tuesday
#TalktomeTuesday – What is the relationship you've worked the hardest for and had the best outcome?

_____
_____

Wednesday
1. _____
2. _____
3. _____

When the search for truth becomes a celebration of being, all of life transforms on its own.

-Matt Kahn

Thursday

1. _____
2. _____
3. _____

Friday

1. _____
2. _____
3. _____

Saturday

1. _____
2. _____
3. _____

Sunday

1. _____
2. _____
3. _____

The BEST thing that happened in my life this week was:

_____
_____
_____

I have now completed _____ **weeks of practicing gratitude!**

(cross off completed weeks with a brightly-colored pen)

1	2	3	4	5
6	7	8	9	
10	11	12		
13	Lifestyle...			

My favorite part of this journey has been:

_____

_____

_____

_____

I notice changes in the way I:

_____

_____

_____

_____

Week 9

WEEK 9 _____ to _____

This week I am most excited about:

_____

_____

_____

"Today, I am grateful for…"

Monday
1. _____
2. _____
3. _____

Tuesday
#TalktomeTuesday – What made you laugh the most in your childhood?

_____

_____

Wednesday
1. _____
2. _____
3. _____

Gratitude is not only the greatest of all virtues, but the parent of all others.

-Cicero

Thursday

1. _____
2. _____
3. _____

Friday

1. _____
2. _____
3. _____

Saturday

1. _____
2. _____
3. _____

Sunday

1. _____
2. _____
3. _____

The BEST thing that happened in my life this week was:

_____
_____
_____

I am grateful to be **ME** because:

1. I like my: _____.

2. I excel at: _____.

3. I bless people often by: _____.

4. I make a special effort to: _____.

5. I am unique because: _____.

Feeling full gratitude for the many gifts that make us who we are allows us to make decisions which honor our integrity and wellbeing.

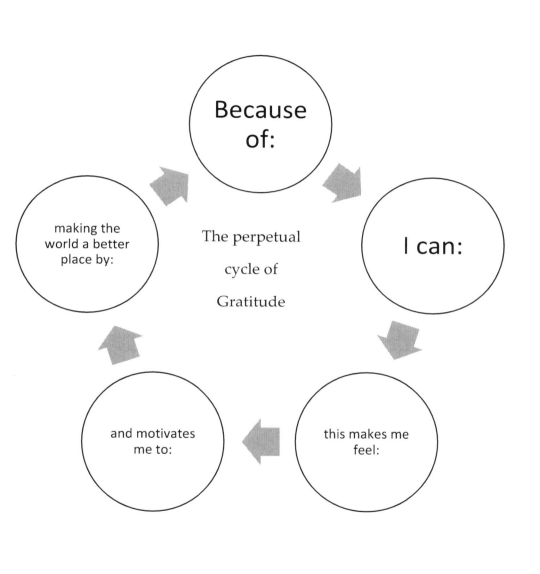

Week 10

WEEK 10　　　_____ to _____

This week I am most excited about:

_____
_____
_____

"Today, I am grateful for…"

Monday
1. _____
2. _____
3. _____

Tuesday
#TalktomeTuesday – What makes you laugh the most in adulthood?
_____
_____

Wednesday
1. _____
2. _____
3. _____

Gratitude is the healthiest of all human emotions.

-Zig Ziglar

Thursday
1. _____
2. _____
3. _____

Friday
1. _____
2. _____
3. _____

Saturday
1. _____
2. _____
3. _____

Sunday
1. _____
2. _____
3. _____

The BEST thing that happened in my life this week was:

_____
_____
_____

Gratitude Reflection

Reflection in meditation is an important part of cultivating awareness of self. The practice of channeling your authenticity can enhance your sense of well-being and both validate and activate your inner guide.

A mindful reflection of Gratitude:

1. Settle yourself in a relaxed posture. Take a few deep, calming breaths to relax and center. Inhale deeply and exhale slowly. Let your attention retreat, and take awareness of all things sensory. What can you smell, taste, touch, see, and hear?

   Say to yourself: "For this, I am grateful."

2. Next, call to mind those people in your life with whom you are closest: your friends, family, partner.

   Say to yourself, "For them, I am grateful."

3. Next, focus your attention to your internal being – your Inner Guide. Your authentic self is blessed with imagination, communication skills, to learn from the past and plan for the future, and to overcome any obstacle or pain you may be experiencing.

   Say to yourself: "For this, I am grateful."

4. Finally, take a deep breath and exhale in the realization that life is a precious. Acknowledge that you have been born into a period of immense prosperity. Remember that you are a spiritual being having a physical experience and have been given the gift of health, culture, and access to spiritual teachings.

   Say to yourself: "For this, I am grateful."

Week 11

WEEK 11 _____ to _____

This week I am most excited about:

_____

_____

_____

"Today, I am grateful for…"

Monday

1. _____

2. _____

3. _____

Tuesday

#TalktomeTuesday – When was the last time you experienced a blessing in disguise?

_____

_____

Wednesday

1. _____

2. _____

3. _____

Gratitude opens the door to the power, the wisdom, the creativity of the universe.

-Deepak Chopra

Thursday
1._____
2._____
3._____

Friday
1._____
2._____
3._____

Saturday
1._____
2._____
3._____

Sunday
1._____
2._____
3._____

The BEST thing that happened in my life this week was:
_____
_____
_____

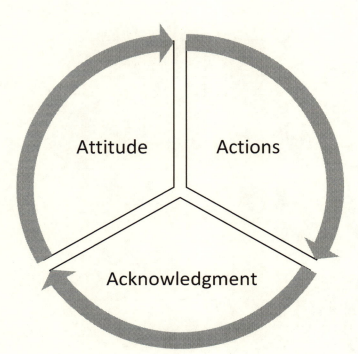

Change Agents for Self-Improvement

If you improve yourself by one percent each day, you will have improved <u>365%</u> after one year.

Week 12

WEEK 12 _____ to _____

This week I am most excited about:
_____
_____
_____

"Today, I am grateful for…"

Monday
1. _____
2. _____
3. _____

Tuesday
#TalktomeTuesday – Most recent non-tangible gift someone has given you?
_____
_____

Wednesday
1. _____
2. _____
3. _____

You have no cause for anything but gratitude and joy.

-Buddha

Thursday
1. _____
2. _____
3. _____

Friday
1. _____
2. _____
3. _____

Saturday
1. _____
2. _____
3. _____

Sunday
1. _____
2. _____
3. _____

The BEST thing that happened in my life this week was:

_____
_____
_____

Gratitude Jar

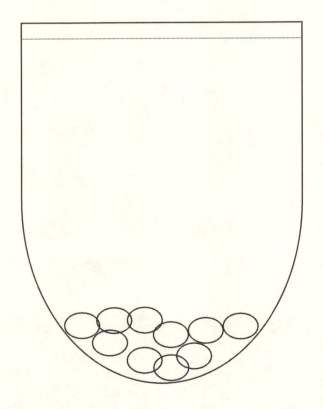

You're nearly a pro!

Help inspire the rest of your household with a gratitude jar.

HERE'S WHAT YOU NEED:

Flat decorative marbles (light colored) *

2 mason jars or vases

Fine-tipped Sharpie

HERE'S WHAT YOU DO:

Keep a jar of blank marbles next to your Gratitude Jar.

When someone notices or expresses gratitude for something, write that act/object/feeling on the marble and transfer it to the other jar.

When the jar is full of marked marbles, schedule a special date and share a treat while you all review your Thankfuls together!

*small slips of paper/popsicle sticks/many craft items can be used for this. The intention is to create a visual representation of gratitude filling your home.

Week 13

WEEK 13 _____ to _____

This week I am most excited about:

_____

_____

_____

"Today, I am grateful for…"

Monday
1. _____
2. _____
3. _____

Tuesday
#TalktomeTuesday – How have you shared your abundance this week?

_____

_____

Wednesday
1. _____
2. _____
3. _____

A grateful heart is a magnet for miracles.

-Unknown

Thursday

1._____
2._____
3._____

Friday

1._____
2._____
3._____

Saturday

1._____
2._____
3._____

Sunday

1._____
2._____
3._____

The BEST thing that happened in my life this week was:

_____
_____
_____

YOU DID IT!

90 days of giving thanks for both big and small things in your life.

Now, reflect.

Open your journal to a random page, and read about your week. How does this make you feel? Can you name the emotions that are surfacing?

_____

_____

_____

Ninety days doesn't seem like a long time, but it is a *quarter of a year*. If you spend too many quarters of a year without happiness, they begin to add up to whole years. Life is too short to spend whole years unhappy.

Compare your contentment today to your state of being a quarter of a year ago. Do you feel more, or less satisfaction with your being today? Do you experience more hope, joy, and laughter than you did 90 days ago?

_____

_____

_____

Notes

Notes

Notes

Notes

Notes

Notes

Notes

Notes

Notes

Notes

Notes

Notes

Notes

Notes

Notes

Notes

Notes

Notes

Notes

About the Author

Gina Low is a mom, wife, kid-sports cheerleader, and wine taster who swears that the *40s* are the best years of her life – because, *Gratitude*.

She writes *She's Overflowing* for all you fellow warriors who may have temporarily lost yourselves in the throes of spit up and goldfish. She will help guide you through the years of cleats, cups (every cup but sippy cups anymore), and collective bargaining with teens; all while reminding you that your oxygen mask must come first.

Join Gina and the rest of the #gratitudegang at www.she'soverflowing.com!

Made in the USA
San Bernardino, CA
17 May 2019